This Book Belongs To

Dear diary, today I felt...

Notes

Notes

I am Proud of myself for all the times I kept going

Dear diary, today I felt...

Notes

Notes

I am Proud of myself for all the times I kept going

Dear diary, today I felt...

Notes

Notes

I am Proud of myself for all the times I kept going

Dear diary, today I felt...

Notes

Notes

I am Proud of myself for all the times I kept going

Dear diary, today I felt...

Notes

Notes

Dear diary, today I felt... 

Notes

Notes

I am Proud of myself for all the times I kept going

Dear diary, today I felt...

Notes

Notes

I am Proud of myself for all the times I kept going

Dear diary, today I felt...

Notes

Notes

Dear diary, today I felt...

Notes

Notes

I am Proud of myself for all the times I kept going

Dear diary, today I felt...

Notes

Notes

I am Proud of myself for all the times I kept going

Dear diary, today I felt...

Notes

Notes

I am Proud of myself for all the times I kept going

Dear diary, today I felt...

Notes

Notes

I am Proud of myself for all the times I kept going

Dear diary, today I felt...

Notes

Notes

I am Proud of myself for all the times I kept going

Dear diary, today I felt...

Notes

Notes

I am Proud of myself for all the times I kept going

Dear diary, today I felt...

Notes

Notes

I am Proud of myself for all the times I kept going

Dear diary, today I felt...

Notes

Notes

I am Proud of myself for all the times I kept going

Dear diary, today I felt...

Notes

Notes

I am Proud of myself for all the times I kept going

Dear diary, today I felt...

Notes

Notes

I am Proud of myself for all the times I kept going

Dear diary, today I felt...

Notes

Notes

I am Proud of myself for all the times I kept going

Dear diary, today I felt...

Notes

Notes

Dear diary, today I felt... ✻

Notes   Notes

I am Proud of myself for all the times I kept going

Dear diary, today I felt...

Notes

Notes

I am Proud of myself for all the times I kept going

Dear diary, today I felt...

Notes

Notes

I am Proud of myself for all the times I kept going

Dear diary, today I felt... 

Notes

Notes

I am Proud of myself for all the times I kept going

Dear diary, today I felt...

____
____
____
____
____
____
____
____
____
____

Notes

Notes

I am Proud of myself for all the times I kept going

Dear diary, today I felt...

Notes

Notes

I am Proud of myself for all the times I kept going

Dear diary, today I felt...

Notes

Notes

Dear diary, today I felt...

Notes

Notes

I am Proud of myself for all the times I kept going

Dear diary, today I felt...

Notes

Notes

I am Proud of myself for all the times I kept going

Dear diary, today I felt...

Notes

Notes

I am Proud of myself for all the times I kept going

Dear diary, today I felt...

Notes

Notes

Dear diary, today I felt...

Notes

Notes

I am Proud of myself for all the times I kept going

Dear diary, today I felt...

Notes

Notes

I am Proud of myself for all the times I kept going

Dear diary, today I felt...

Notes

Notes

I am Proud of myself for all the times I kept going

Dear diary, today I felt...

____

____

____

____

____

____

____

____

____

____

Notes

Notes

I am Proud of myself for all the times I kept going

Dear diary, today I felt...

Notes

Notes

I am Proud of myself for all the times I kept going

Dear diary, today I felt...

Notes

Notes

I am Proud of myself for all the times I kept going

Dear diary, today I felt...

Notes

Notes

I am Proud of myself for all the times I kept going

Dear diary, today I felt...

I am Proud of myself for all the times I kept going

Dear diary, today I felt...

Notes

Notes

I am Proud of myself for all the times I kept going

Dear diary, today I felt...

Notes

Notes

I am Proud of myself for all the times I kept going

Dear diary, today I felt...

Notes

Notes

I am Proud of myself for all the times I kept going

Dear diary, today I felt...

Notes

Notes

I am Proud of myself for all the times I kept going

Dear diary, today I felt...

Notes

Notes

I am Proud of myself for all the times I kept going

Dear diary, today I felt...

Notes

Notes

I am Proud of myself for all the times I kept going

Dear diary, today I felt...

Notes

Notes

Dear diary, today I felt...

Notes

Notes

I am Proud of myself for all the times I kept going

Dear diary, today I felt...

Notes

Notes

I am Proud of myself for all the times I kept going

Dear diary, today I felt...

Notes

Notes

I am Proud of myself for all the times I kept going

Dear diary, today I felt...

Notes

Notes

I am Proud of myself for all the times I kept going

Dear diary, today I felt...

Notes

Notes

Dear diary, today I felt...

Notes

Notes

I am Proud of myself for all the times I kept going

Dear diary, today I felt...

Notes

Notes

I am Proud of myself for all the times I kept going

Dear diary, today I felt...

Notes

Notes

Dear diary, today I felt...

Notes

Notes

I am Proud of myself for all the times I kept going

Dear diary, today I felt...

Notes

Notes

I am Proud of myself for all the times I kept going

Dear diary, today I felt...

Notes

Notes

I am Proud of myself for all the times I kept going

Dear diary, today I felt...

Notes

Notes

I am Proud of myself for all the times I kept going

Dear diary, today I felt...

Notes

Notes

I am Proud of myself for all the times I kept going

Dear diary, today I felt...

____

____

____

____

____

____

____

____

____

Notes

Notes

I am Proud of myself for all the times I kept going

Dear diary, today I felt...

Notes

Notes

Dear diary, today I felt...

____

____

____

____

____

____

____

____

____

Notes

Notes

I am Proud of myself for all the times I kept going

Dear diary, today I felt...

Notes

Notes

I am Proud of myself for all the times I kept going

Dear diary, today I felt...

Notes

Notes

I am Proud of myself for all the times I kept going

Dear diary, today I felt...

Notes

Notes

I am Proud of myself for all the times I kept going

Dear diary, today I felt... 

I am Proud of myself for all the times I kept going

Dear diary, today I felt...

Notes

Notes

I am Proud of myself for all the times I kept going

Dear diary, today I felt...

Notes

Notes

I am Proud of myself for all the times I kept going

Dear diary, today I felt...

Dear diary, today I felt...

Notes

Notes

Dear diary, today I felt...

Notes

Notes

I am Proud of myself for all the times I kept going

Dear diary, today I felt...

Notes

Notes

I am Proud of myself for all the times I kept going

Dear diary, today I felt...

Notes

Notes

I am Proud of myself for all the times I kept going

Dear diary, today I felt...

Notes

Notes

I am Proud of myself for all the times I kept going

Dear diary, today I felt...

Notes

Notes

Dear diary, today I felt...

Notes

Notes

I am Proud of myself for all the times I kept going

Dear diary, today I felt...

Notes

Notes

I am Proud of myself for all the times I kept going

Dear diary, today I felt...

Notes

Notes

I am Proud of myself for all the times I kept going

Dear diary, today I felt...

Notes

Notes

I am Proud of myself for all the times I kept going

Dear diary, today I felt...

Notes

Notes

I am Proud of myself for all the times I kept going

Dear diary, today I felt...

____

____

____

____

____

____

____

____

____

Notes

Notes

I am Proud of myself for all the times I kept going

Dear diary, today I felt...

Notes

Notes

I am Proud of myself for all the times I kept going

Dear diary, today I felt...

Notes

Notes

I am Proud of myself for all the times I kept going

Dear diary, today I felt...

Notes

Notes

Dear diary, today I felt...

Notes

Notes

I am Proud of myself for all the times I kept going

Dear diary, today I felt...

Notes

Notes

I am Proud of myself for all the times I kept going

Dear diary, today I felt...

Notes

Notes

I am Proud of myself for all the times I kept going

Dear diary, today I felt...

Notes

Notes

Dear diary, today I felt...

Notes

Notes

Dear diary, today I felt...

Notes

Notes

I am Proud of myself for all the times I kept going

Dear diary, today I felt...

Notes

Notes

I am Proud of myself for all the times I kept going

Dear diary, today I felt...

Notes

Notes

I am Proud of myself for all the times I kept going

Dear diary, today I felt...

Notes

Notes

I am Proud of myself for all the times I kept going

Dear diary, today I felt...

Notes

Notes

I am Proud of myself for all the times I kept going

Dear diary, today I felt...

Notes

Notes

I am Proud of myself for all the times I kept going

Dear diary, today I felt...

Notes

Notes

I am Proud of myself for all the times I kept going

Dear diary, today I felt...

Notes

Notes

I am Proud of myself for all the times I kept going

Dear diary, today I felt...

Notes

Notes

I am Proud of myself for all the times I kept going

Dear diary, today I felt...

Notes

Notes

I am Proud of myself for all the times I kept going